Original title:

The Journey to Life's Purpose (Not a Smooth Ride)

Copyright © 2025 Creative Arts Management OÜ
All rights reserved.

Author: Liam Sterling
ISBN HARDBACK: 978-1-80566-161-0
ISBN PAPERBACK: 978-1-80566-456-7

Pilgrimage of the Heart

I packed my snacks and silly hats,
For what I thought, were easy chats.
But every road, it twisted wide,
And laughter met me as my guide.

I tripped on rocks, I danced in rain,
With muddy boots, a hint of pain.
Yet with each tumble, giggles grew,
For purpose found me, bright and new.

The Mapless Expedition

I set out once with a broom and a mop,
Thought life's backroads would be a hop.
But turns out I took a left, not right,
And ended up at a cat's surprise night.

I met a goat who offered tips,
He chewed my map while doing flips.
Now I wander bold, with no GPS,
Just follow the snacks, no more stress!

Echoes of Hope in Stormy Seas

I sailed a boat made of jellybeans,
Hoping to reach what destiny means.
But waves went splashing, chaos rang,
I learned to swim, and even sang.

The seagulls laughed 'til they turned blue,
When I chased fish that slipped right through.
Yet every splash was full of cheer,
Oh, lesson learned, keep laughter near!

The Uncharted Ascent

I climbed a hill that had no peak,
And talked to rocks, felt rather geek.
The path was steep, my legs were sore,
But then I found a dozen more!

I raised a flag – it was a sock,
Claimed victory atop that block.
And though the climb was quite absurd,
I found my joy, it's plain and heard.

Chasing Whispers of Meaning

I set out one sunny day,
With socks mismatched and hair at play.
I thought I'd find wisdom, profound and bright,
Instead, I lost my way in a kite fight.

A map in hand, I wandered proud,
But what I sought was lost in the crowd.
Turns out, the answers were just a gleam,
Bouncing around like a playful dream.

Navigating Life's Rough Waters

I sailed on a boat, all shiny and new,
With a parrot named Larry, who just loves to chew.
We hit every wave like it was a dance,
And swabbed the deck with little chance.

The compass spun wild, the stars wouldn't show,
I asked Larry, 'Where are we supposed to go?'
He squawked, 'Just enjoy it, stop fussing, dear!'
So we sailed off course with plenty of cheer.

Turning The Page in Uncertainty

I opened a book, it was upside down,
The words laughed at me, what a silly clown!
Each chapter a puzzle, each plot did twirl,
I glanced at the cover and gave it a whirl.

A twist here, a turn there, I stumbled along,
Found I was dancing to a nonsensical song.
I flipped through the pages, made quite a scene,
For life, my dear friends, is hardly routine.

Milestones Amidst the Shadows

I marked my milestones in chalk on the street,
Dancing with shadows, oh what a feat!
Each step felt wobbly, like juggling pies,
Yet laughter erupted from deep down inside.

There are bumps on the road, yes, and some mud,
But through giggles and stumbles, I found my own bud.
So here's to the chaos, the mess, and the fun,
Life's purpose, I get it, is to be number one!

Constellations of Purpose Amidst the Clouds

Up above, stars twinkle bright,
They laugh at our plight,
While we trip on rocks,
Searching for clocks.

Clouds float by, soft and wide,
Nudging dreams, taking them for a ride,
With each step, a twist of fate,
Did I mention I'm always late?

The map's a riddle, lost in time,
My compass keeps dancing, it's quite a crime,
Navigating paths with a goofy smile,
Who knew chaos could be such a style?

Yet in this mess, I chase my dreams,
Falling flat, or so it seems,
Through laughter and tears, I find my grace,
In every stumble, there's a funny face.

Raindrops on Dusty Paths

Raindrops tap on dusty shoes,
Squishing mud, I can't refuse,
Splashing puddles, oh what fun,
Life's a canvas, we're all the sun.

I slip and slide, it's quite the show,
Creating rain dances, in a row,
Umbrellas flipped inside out, oh dear,
Still, I chuckle, not one fear.

With every step, the world's a joke,
Chasing giggles as I croak,
Life's a slippery circus, no doubt,
But I'm the clown, laughing out loud.

In puddles, I find reflective dreams,
Drowning worries in playful schemes,
Through every raindrop, I shall tread,
Finding joy where less was said.

Pathways of Uncertainty

On this path, I skip and hop,
With no clue where I'll stop,
Laughter echoes in each misstep,
Trusting fate with each last rep.

The signs are wobbly, a total mess,
But hey, who goes less is more, I guess,
Around each bend, a surprise awaits,
Maybe it's cake, or just empty plates.

I navigate with a goofy grin,
Bumping into trees, what a win,
Through valleys low and hills so steep,
I tumble, rumble, and hope to leap.

Yet in this puzzle, I rise and fall,
Embracing the chaos, I'll stand tall,
For in every twist, life holds delight,
Dancing through shadows, laughing at night.

Chasing Shadows of Intent

Shadows tease beneath the sun,
Chasing dreams that weigh a ton,
I hop and skip, give it a whirl,
In this grand game, I'm just the girl.

Every corner hides a clue,
Mismatched socks, is that a view?
I trip on thoughts, they scatter wide,
Yet each hiccup, I take with pride.

Intentions swirl like leaves in breeze,
Whirling past with such great ease,
I laugh at plans that go astray,
Finding joy in the silly play.

Through tangled paths, and silly fates,
I twirl and dance, no room for hates,
In chasing shadows, I glow so bright,
Life's a jest; I dance into the night.

Forks Behind Misty Pines

In the woods where frogs hold court,
My GPS went out, I fell short.
Took a left, then a quick right,
Now I'm chasing squirrels in flight.

The path ahead looks like a maze,
I follow a trail of lost sayings.
A sign says 'Don't feed the baboons',
But here they are playing harpoons!

Under trees with faces that stare,
I trip on roots, feeling quite bare.
Misty pines hide secrets unseen,
Like my last meal and that big green bean!

At every fork, laughter ensues,
Who knew I'd require hiking shoes?
With each step, I dance in a swirl,
Life's purpose? It's just a fun twirl!

The Pulse of Possibility

With a pulse as fast as a caffeinated squirrel,
I dash down paths where dreams unfurl.
Every twist has a punchline's spark,
Flip a coin; let's get this arc!

I tried to juggle all my grand hopes,
But ended up tripping on floating ropes.
The sky can be blue or a deep shade of grey,
But watch for the gumballs that come out to play!

Dodging pitfalls, I laugh through the mess,
Life's a game show, I'm feeling blessed.
Do I win a stuffed llama or a peach?
Either way, I'm learning to stretch and reach.

Each stumble's a giggle, a tickle of fate,
Finding purpose like it's not too late.
With every misstep, I take off my frown,
On this wild ride, I'm the fun-loving clown!

Silent Rivers of Reflection

By the river where silence takes a nap,
I ponder my purpose, then wear a cap.
The fish start laughing, they whisper in bliss,
What's life without a splash of fishy kiss?

On rocky banks, I trip on my thoughts,
Fishing for wisdom, connecting the dots.
What's my goal? A big, tall tree?
Or sneaking cupcakes, just to feel free?

Ripples spin tales as they make their way,
I wave back, hoping they'll stay.
Each wisdom drop feels like a prank,
Should I build a raft or start a bank?

Through chuckles and giggles, I float along,
With the current, I know I belong.
In the silence, I find quite a score,
Purpose is laughter, shoes by the door!

Sparks from the Forge

In a forge where ideas clash and collide,
I hammer away with mischief as my guide.
A plan comes out like a hot, twisted mess,
Yet somehow I'm feeling quite blessed!

With every spark that leaps to the air,
I juggle hopes, looks like flair!
The anvil's singing a tune quite funny,
Is life about gold or a pile of honey?

My hands are tired, my mind in a spin,
But oh what a dance this chaotic din!
Each misfire is comedy, bright and bold,
Creating something that can't be sold.

As sparks fade, I laugh with delight,
Purpose found under the moonlight.
This forge of life, with its clinks and chimes,
Is filled with giggles, tangled rhymes!

Serendipity in the Mist

Woke up late, coffee's gone,
Chasing dreams with a croissant.
My map is blank, but who needs one?
Found a cat, now we're having fun.

Laughed at clouds, they looked so gray,
Chased a rainbow, lost my way.
Met a squirrel, shared a nut,
He winked at me, said, "What's up?"

Hit a puddle, splashed about,
Pants are wet, I scream and shout.
Laughter echoes through the street,
Life's surprises taste so sweet.

In the mist, lost but not sad,
Every stumble makes me glad.
Serendipity's my best mate,
With a smile, I carry fate.

Battles on the Prairie

Once a knight, now I'm a fan,
Defending donuts from a can.
Stingy seagulls, fierce and sly,
Making off with my apple pie.

On the prairie, fields of woe,
Battled weeds that wouldn't go.
A tumbleweed rolled in to cheer,
And laughed at all my pesky fears.

I mounted my trusty lawn chair,
To scout the horizon with flair.
But a breeze knocked me to the ground,
While laughter echoed all around.

Victory dances with your snacks,
Life's a circus with no tracks.
In these battles, don't forget,
A sense of humor's the best bet.

Shattered Maps of Meaning

Maps all torn, ink's a blur,
Finding meaning is a stir.
Got a compass that's upside down,
Life's a puzzle all around.

Chasing dreams in a blindfold,
Thoughts are scattered, tales unfold.
A road sign points to 'Who Knows Where?'
Got lost again, but I don't care.

Met a llama wearing shades,
Gave me advice, said, "Don't be afraid!"
Shattered maps can still be fun,
With laughter ringing like a drum.

Journey's not set in stone,
Just grab a snack and roam.
With every twist, a wink and cheer,
Life's a comic, never fear.

Twists and Turns of Existence

Round and round, the path is kooky,
Life's a dance, sometimes spooky.
Found a giraffe stuck in a tree,
He said, "Life's absurd, just like me!"

Tangled vines are not a foe,
They lead to places we don't know.
I took a step, tripped on a rock,
A tumble caught me like a clock.

In this maze, I twirl and spin,
Unexpected joys found within.
With a clown shoe on my feet,
I pirouette, the world's a treat.

Sure, the route can feel erratic,
But laughter makes it democratic.
Twists and turns, bring on the fun,
Existence shines, and I've just begun.

Roads Less Traveled

I took a path less traveled right,
With twists and turns, oh what a sight!
I tripped on roots and dodged a deer,
And found a squirrel who barked with cheer.

The sign said 'this way, you can't go wrong,'
But all it led to was a karaoke song.
I sang my heart out, quite out of tune,
While birds laughed hard, like a cartoon!

I met a frog who claimed to be wise,
With a crown made of leaves, a big surprise!
He said, 'To find purpose, hop real high,'
I jumped so far, I touched the sky!

But then I fell, oh what a crash,
Landed in mud with a thunderous splash!
Yet here I stand, caked in gunk,
Life's silly ride, I must admit, is funk!

Whispers of Destiny

I sought a sign, a whispered plea,
But all I got was a buzzing bee!
It danced around with flaps so loud,
I lost my path and wept aloud.

A fortune teller said, 'You'll shine!'
But all I found was poor old wine.
I thought a party beckoned near,
Instead, found me in pajamas here!

With cards laid out, I'm on a quest,
Of all the choices, which is best?
Answer me now, oh twisty fate,
Just don't send me to a blind date!

I tripped on luck like a misplaced sock,
And bumped my head on a ticking clock.
Yet laughter lights the bumps we face,
In life's grand show, we all have our place!

Navigating Stormy Seas

Set sail for dreams on a rickety boat,
With oars made of spaghetti—what a note!
Waves of doubt tried to capsize me,
But I just grip and giggle with glee!

A seagull squawked, 'You'll never find land!'
I tossed him a chip, he joined my band.
Together we danced on turbulent tides,
With laughter the compass, we took wild rides!

The stormy skies brewed a thunderous show,
I sang 'I Will Survive' with gusto, you know!
The clouds just chuckled, they had no fear,
When life gets rough, just bring good cheer!

So here I float on this noodle of fate,
With every wave, I just celebrate.
Though seas may be restless, I'll steer with pride,
For the winds of humor are my true guide!

Beneath the Veil of Ambition

I wore ambition like a fancy hat,
It looked so grand, but oh, what of that?
With dreams that glimmered, like stars at night,
But behind the scenes? What a silly sight!

I tried to climb success, up a steep hill,
But slipped on optimism, what a thrill!
I tumbled down, like a rolling stone,
And knocked over goals I thought I'd own!

A friend called to say, 'Let's make a plan,'
I brought confetti, he brought a fan.
We celebrated failures with funky tunes,
Dancing to setbacks like happy loons!

So if you stumble, don't lose your spark,
Just laugh it off and embrace your quirk.
For life's true purpose, in every strife,
Is finding the joy in this wild life!

Dreams in the Rubble

Once I dreamed of gold and fame,
But tripped on rocks and laughed at shame.
My goal's a lighthouse far away,
Yet here I sit, and eat my clay.

Each misstep paints a tale unique,
Like dancing on a trampoline peak.
With every fall, a grin I wear,
The circus life—I'm almost there!

Shifting Sands of Time

The clock ticks fast, the sand slips through,
I chase my dreams, but oh, who knew?
I've bumbled forth, a comedy show,
Stumbling on paths where I can't go.

Each grain of time, a prankster's grin,
I trip and fall, yet still dive in.
For every laugh, a wisdom gain,
I dance on risks like it's a game!

The Echo of Your Voice

I followed whispers in the breeze,
But lost my way—oh, such degrees!
With echoes bouncing, sharp and low,
I laughed out loud, it stole the show.

In every word, a riddle spun,
Each hint I chased became such fun!
With every call, a laugh was thrown,
I guess I'm never quite alone.

Celestial Clues

The stars above, they joke with me,
As I search for signs, quite carelessly.
Constellations laugh, they wink and tease,
I think I'll find my path—if you please!

Each twinkle shines with silly glee,
Leading me where I can't quite see.
With cosmic hints like clownish winks,
I'll dance my way, and fill the blanks!

The Relentless Climb

Up the hill we laugh and groan,
Wishing for a comfy throne.
With each step, shoes feel tight,
Yet here we are, giving it a fight.

Rocks and roots are all around,
One wrong step, and down we bound.
Sipping water, dodging bees,
Life's a circus, if you please!

Leaning back, we take a break,
Spot a snack — is that a flake?
Fruits and nuts we hoard in packs,
But chips will lay our courage lax!

Finally, we reach the top,
But wait! Is that a soda pop?
Cheers to the climb, we toast in cheer,
To life's wild ride, let's make it clear!

Storms and Sunbursts on the Road

Clouds roll in, a cheeky grin,
Raindrops dance, let the fun begin!
Umbrellas flip, we laugh and play,
Who knew storms could brighten the day?

Sunshine breaks, with rays so bright,
Time to dry off, what a sight!
We toss our wet shoes far away,
Who needs 'em? We'll barefoot today!

Puddles splash, we leap and yell,
Each tiny wave casts a spell.
Driving through life's ups and downs,
With laughter painted in our frowns.

With every squall and sunny hue,
We chase the rainbows, me and you.
Life's a ride, so full of cheer,
With storms and sunbursts, we persevere!

Shadows Dancing with Light

In corners dark, shadows creep,
We tickle them; they giggle and leap.
A flutter here, a little dance,
Under the glow, they spin and prance.

Light flickers, casting their fate,
Belly laughs with a side of fate.
Chasing giggles, we play tag,
Life's a documentary, no drag!

A shadow stretched, oh what a sight,
On my wall, it gives a fright.
Yet with a wiggle and a shake,
Even shadows just want a break!

So let's embrace the shades we meet,
They lighten up the life we greet.
Together we'll dance, in the dark or bright,
In every moment lies delight!

Reflections from the Edge of Chaos

Standing here on the edge we sway,
Reflecting life in a quirky way.
Chaos reigns, oh what a mess,
We sip tea, while we assess!

Flipping coins, will it be heads?
Or is it tails where chaos treads?
We juggle dreams, like pies in the air,
Who knew life's a circus? Beware!

In the swirl of chaos, we might find,
That laughter heals the worried mind.
With every tumble, slip, and fall,
We gather joy — the best of all.

Thus we stand, with grace and ease,
Amidst the wind, we dance and tease.
Reflections shine from the chaos inside,
In every hiccup, let's take pride!

Serpentine Paths

Winding roads with twists and turns,
You might see goats and a clown that yearns.
A map in hand, but directions unclear,
Laughing at signs that disappear.

Left was right, but not the case,
I drove around in a rabbit's chase.
A shortcut taken, but oh, what a plight,
Stuck in a field, lost in twilight.

Beneath the Surface of Certainty

Underneath this calm facade,
Lies chaos, like a jovial bard.
Certainty dances, then trips on a vine,
Poking fun at plans that decline.

With steadfast steps in a wobbly shoe,
I marched ahead, thinking I knew.
But every certainty just made me laugh,
Like a cat trying to swim in a giraffe.

Heartbeats in the Unpredictable

With every beat, my heart skips a thought,
Like a fish on land that's awkwardly caught.
Plans made for brunch, but lunch is a dive,
Where laughs get tangled, and surprises arrive.

The clock ticks, but what's the time?
Is this a journey or a rhythm and rhyme?
Yet through the chaos, I find my beat,
Grooving along with life's funny tweet.

The Music of Misdirection

A melody plays, but wrong is the key,
Dancing to tunes that just aren't for me.
Every wrong turn has its own little song,
Like a cat that thinks it can do the cha-cha all along.

Notes that clash, then suddenly blend,
Misdirected paths, with laughter to lend.
In this symphony of life so absurd,
I find joy in every confused word.

Beyond the Bend

I took a left at crazy town,
Turning dreams upside down.
With a map made of spaghetti,
I tripped on a funny confetti.

They said follow the trail, it's bright,
But all I found was a cat in fright.
Chasing butterflies on the way,
I lost a shoe, oh what a day!

Each step I took feels mostly wrong,
But the laughs keep me pushing along.
With every bump, a giggle is found,
Guess life's a circus, wildly unbound.

So onward I go with a grin so wide,
Embracing each tumble, each slide.
Like a rollercoaster, who knows the end?
Just here for the laughter, my utmost friend.

The Cost of Clarity

I bought my dreams at a yard sale,
Wore them all like a funny tail.
Each dream was a size too small,
But I strutted like I owned it all.

With a clear head and muddy feet,
Found clarity dancing in defeat.
Can't find the path if it's too neat,
I'll follow the crumbs of a day-old treat.

They say wisdom comes with a fee,
But I traded mine for a cup of tea.
Sipped on doubts, chewed on fears,
While laughter drowned the bitter tears.

So here am I, a dime store sage,
Navigating life like a funny stage.
For every mishap that comes my way,
I'll take it lightly, come what may.

Uncharted Destinies

They told me, 'Go left, it's wise,'
But I flipped a coin and met surprise.
Found a parade of dancing socks,
And a rubber chicken that surely talks.

In the quest for future fate,
Found a sign that read, 'Just wait!'
Did a jig and spun around,
Laughter echoed, a goofy sound.

Each misstep leads to the best of times,
Tripped over dreams, stumbled on rhymes.
If life hands you lemons so sour,
Just juggle them, add some flour!

With no map to guide the way,
I'm drawn to silliness like it's a play.
Though the road's a puzzle, all jumbled and wild,
I'll dance through the chaos, a happy child.

Kaleidoscope of Ambitions

A thought popped up like a balloon,
Wobbled around like a kooky cartoon.
Colors swirling in a laugh parade,
Each vision a joke that just won't fade.

Wrote plans in whipped cream, like a dream,
But it melted fast, not as it seemed.
Chased a shadow, I thought was gold,
Turns out it was my sock's mate, bold!

I googled 'life' but got cat memes,
Perhaps that's how ambition gleams.
With every twist, new colors arise,
Creating a palette of surprised eyes.

So here I stand with a fumble and flair,
Embracing life's quirks with humor to spare.
In this kaleidoscope, I'll find my way,
Laughing through colors, come what may.

Maps Made of Stardust

I bought a map made of stardust,
But it led me straight to a bust.
With every twist, a little fray,
I thought I'd find a shortcut way.

I navigated clouds and laughter,
Chasing dreams that went much faster.
Found a coffee shop on Mars,
But the barista served me stars.

The GPS said, 'Recalculating!'
As I danced with fate, hearts palpitating.
Each wrong turn, a silly delight,
Who knew the cosmos could be so bright?

So here I wander, map in hand,
With stardust grains as my travel band.
With every skip and hop and bump,
I find my joy in every jump.

Shadows of Intention

I set out with grand intention,
But tripped over my own invention.
Shadows danced in your direction,
Whispering notes of disconnection.

"Hey there, friend!" I called aloud,
Only to bump a passing cloud.
It showered me with moonlit sprinkles,
Should I jump or run or crinkle?

Each step I took was filled with flair,
With wobbly wishes, I lost my hair!
Yet laughter echoed on the way,
As I stumbled through the light of day.

With shadows laughing in my wake,
A journey's path, this silly snake.
Embracing chaos, I'll persist,
For life's a joy, how could I resist?

Guiding Lights of Grit

I followed lights, all shiny and bright,
Thought they'd guide me to the right sight.
But every step, I lost my place,
A disco ball in a cosmic race.

With grit in hand, I danced along,
To beats of life, a quirky song.
I moonwalked past the trees and stones,
Each misstep echoed silly groans!

Illusions flickered like fireflies,
Twinkling tales of grand surprise.
But as I stumbled, fell, and rolled,
I found true fun's worth more than gold.

So I embrace these guiding lights,
With laughter blazing through the nights.
For every falter on this spree,
Reveals a truth: I'm truly free.

Choices in the Twilight

In twilight hours, choices swirl,
Like candy-coated dreams that twirl.
I picked a path that led me wrong,
But found a flower with a groovy song.

Do I turn left or spin around?
Each twist and turn, joy can be found.
But even as I fumble and trip,
Life feeds me chocolate on this trip.

With every glance at what I chose,
I laughed at how a door just froze.
For in the chaos, I start to see,
That choices lead to who I'll be.

So here I stand, with muddied shoes,
Embracing every bump, every bruise.
Tomorrow greets with fresh new quests,
In twilight's arms, I'm truly blessed.

Footprints on Shifting Sand

I started out with flip-flops on,
A map in hand, feeling strong.
But every step, a twist and turn,
And now my feet seem to adjourn.

The tide comes in, my path's erased,
I chase my thoughts; they've all been laced.
Lost on this beach I thought I knew,
Who knew the sun could bake me too?

The seagulls laugh, they point and squawk,
While I just hope to find a rock.
These footprints made, just a fleeting trace,
In the end, it's all a silly race.

The Labyrinth of Self-Discovery

In a maze of mirrors, I'm on display,
With every turn, I lose my way.
"Who am I?" I question aloud,
As I dodge the crowd and feel quite proud.

I trip on thoughts and tumble low,
Conversations with myself, a real show.
The walls echo back my silly fears,
But laughter drowns them out with cheers.

Through twists and turns, I dance and prance,
In my silly search for a second chance.
The mystery's fun, game on repeat,
Who knew self-discovery could be so sweet?

Winds of Change and Wisdom

The wind blew in like a prankster bold,
Whipping my plans into chaos uncontrolled.
I tried to hold tight to dreams I made,
But they sailed away, I felt betrayed.

With each gust, my hair's a mess,
As I try and try to find success.
A wise man said, "Go with the breeze,"
I yelled right back, "You take it, please!"

The lessons come in the quirky ways,
When life decides to play and play.
So I'll dance with the winds, embrace the ride,
Laugh at the chaos with arms open wide.

Breaking Through Barriers of Fear

Fear stood tall like a sturdy wall,
Telling me I could surely fall.
But I packed my bags and wore a grin,
With a can-do spirit, I started to spin.

I stumbled forward, tripped on doubt,
My courage whispered, "You're not out!"
With every misstep, I found my cheer,
Fear turned to laughter, oh my dear!

I crashed through walls, I laughed out loud,
Turns out failure can gather a crowd.
With every crack, I dance on through,
Who knew barriers could be a zoo?

The Art of Falling Forward

I tripped over my dreams today,
My shoelaces tied in a fray.
Life said, 'Get up, try again!'
But gravity laughed, I fell once again!

With every stumble, I learn anew,
Dancing through chaos, like cats in a zoo.
I'll pirouette on my failures' song,
At least, I'm laughing as things go wrong!

I pack my bags for each epic fall,
A collection of bloopers, isn't that tall?
When I land on my face, it's quite absurd,
Chasing success like it's a flightless bird!

So here's to the bruises that never heal,
They're badges of courage, this is how I feel.
If life's a tumble, I'll roll with grace,
As long as I find my hilarious place!

Unraveled Threads of Fate

I knitted my fate with yarn all wrong,
A scarf turned into a very long song.
With knots and loops that tangled tight,
I'm fashionably late in this yarn fight!

My sweater of dreams began to unwind,
Each stitch a lesson, but I lost my mind.
"Who needs a pattern?" I boldly proclaimed,
Now I'm wearing a vest that's slightly maimed!

The needle of time pricks my silly dreams,
But I'm crafting my future, or so it seems.
With every mistake, I'm weaving delight,
Life's a stitch-up, and I'm doing it right!

So here's to the threads that never align,
A tapestry woven with laughter, divine.
If I can't wear a coat of pure style,
I'll rock my knitting with a goofy smile!

Struggles in the Sunlight

I ventured out to chase the light,
But stumbled hard in plain sight.
My sunglasses slipped, I lost my way,
Now I'm dancing like a disarray!

The sun is bright, my path is bright,
Yet tripping on sneakers feels just right.
With a skip and a hop and a flailing arm,
I'm the clown of the block, bringing charm!

When life threw shade, I wore a grin,
Sunburned wisdom from within.
Each misstep a legend, I'll proudly tell,
How I flourished while I fell!

So let the warmth be my silly guide,
I'll laugh through the blunders I cannot hide.
In the brilliant light, I find my way,
With giggles on the road, come what may!

A Compass of Resilience

My compass spins, oh what a sight,
North, south, east—it's just not right!
With a map that's scribbled in crayon tones,
I'm charting a course through the unknowns!

Through twists and turns, I navigate fun,
Like a pirate lost searching for sun.
My treasure of lessons in a chest of smiles,
Worn like a crown from hilarious trials!

With every wrong turn, I laugh and sing,
Who knew misdirection could be this thing?
I may be lost, but don't shed a tear,
I've got a compass of joy, full of cheer!

So here's to the paths less traveled by,
I'll dance on the roads, don't ask me why.
Life's quirky journey, let's laugh aloud,
Together we stumble, let's make it a crowd!

Surges of Self-Discovery

I set off with a grin, feeling bold,
My map was a puzzle, a sight to behold.
The GPS said, 'Left!' so I took a right,
Now I'm chasing my tail, what a goofy sight!

Wandered through forests, got lost in a mall,
Found socks with weird patterns, my greatest haul.
But every wrong turn made me laugh out loud,
Who knew self-discovery could come with a crowd?

I danced with the squirrels, had tea with a bear,
The wisdom they shared was beyond compare.
With every trip tumbler that tipped on my toes,
I found that my purpose was all about those!

So here I stand, in my mismatched shoes,
With cookie crumbs stuck on my bright, colorful hues.
Life's quirks might trip me, but they make me feel free,
I guess my adventure's just meant to be!

Mountains and Valleys of Aspiration

I climbed a big mountain, my heart full of cheer,
With a backpack of donuts, I held them so dear.
But halfway up, I slipped on a rock,
Now I'm rolling down, like an old ticking clock!

In valleys of doubts, I tiptoed with glee,
Tripped over my hopes, what a sight to see!
Yet laughter echoed as I skidded through mud,
Picking dreams like daisies—what a fun stud!

With poppy seed muffins and music so loud,
I danced on a cliff, feeling totally proud.
Then a strong wind blew, and I lost my cap,
Oh well, more adventure—just take a nap!

These ups and downs shine brighter than gold,
Each stumble and tumble a story retold.
I cherish the lessons behind every fall,
In this wild game of life, I'm having a ball!

Embracing the Unknown

Peeking around corners, what will I find?
A dragon? A kitten? Or maybe some kind?
Each step is a riddle, a chapter unwritten,
With a hat on my head, and a cat that is smitten!

Ventured to places, where the grass isn't green,
With a map drawn by crayons, not quite what I mean.
Tripping on shadows and tickling the sun,
Convinced that this crazy is really quite fun!

In a world full of riddles, I'm dancing in socks,
Pandering to pigeons, and befriending the flocks.
There's a laugh in the chaos, a cheer in the mess,
Each wobble a giggle, each stumble a bless!

So here's to the curves, the twists, and the bends,
With a grin on my face, and a heart that transcends.
Unwrapping life's treasures, with every new day,
Embracing the unknown, come what may!

Lessons in the Dust

I tripped on my shoelace, fell flat on my face,
Dust clouds a-flying in a most clumsy race.
But giggles escaped as I lay in the muck,
Learning that falling can sometimes be luck!

The ants had a meeting, they laughed at my plight,
I joined in their chatter, oh what a delight!
With tiny wise lessons from critters so small,
I found I could rise, and I'd just had a ball!

Each stumble a story, each fall quite a treat,
With humor as armor, I can't stand the heat.
For life's little hiccups are just part of the ride,
In the dust, I find treasures where laughter can hide!

So here's to the flops, and the messes I make,
Each lesson a giggle, a piece of my cake.
For every time I crash, I discover new ways,
To juggle the bumps, and live brighter days!

A Silent Symphony of Struggle

In pursuit of dreams, I trip on my shoelace,
Fumbling through life, a comedic rat race.
Dancing with doubt, I twist and I shout,
While the universe chuckles, filled with no doubt.

Maps drawn in crayon, they guide me astray,
Detours and potholes just brighten my day.
With each funny fail, I learn to embrace,
The slapstick routine of this life's crazy pace.

A comedian's heart as I tumble and spin,
Roiling with laughter from deep down within.
Every misstep spins tales, wild like the breeze,
A silent symphony that puts me at ease.

So let's raise a glass to our messy delight,
A show full of blunders, we're stars of the night.
In laughter, we wander, together we glide,
To the rhythm of struggles, where humor can hide.

The Fire Within

In the heart of chaos, a flicker sparks bright,
Fueling my passion, igniting my flight.
Stumbling through flames, I've got marshmallows too,
Cooking up dreams as the smoke starts to brew.

With a grin on my face, I embrace the wild ride,
Singing off-key with the world as my guide.
The fire within me, oh how it can sizzle,
As I dance in the heat, life's riddles I'll drizzle.

Every hot mess I face, just warms up the charm,
With laughter my armor, I'll raise my alarm.
Through singed edges and sparks, I won't lose my skin,
The funniest tales are the ones born of sin.

So I gather my courage, I gather my glee,
In this fiery circus, I'm wild and I'm free.
Let the flames twirl and twist, let the world laugh at me,
For deep in the chaos is where I find glee.

Stories from the Cradle of Chaos

A toddler at play in a tornado of toys,
My life's a jumble, singing silly joys.
Instead of a roadmap, I've got paper planes,
Every crash and burn jaunt spreads laughter like rains.

Shouting 'Adventure!' while my shoelaces tie,
I trip over dreams, but oh, how I fly!
Giggles erupt from the mess I create,
In the cradle of chaos, I find my fate.

Coffee spills spill like confetti in streams,
As I juggle my hopes wrapped in whimsical dreams.
A parade of missteps leads to a sweet cheer,
The best kinds of stories are born from my fear.

So here's to the clowns in the circus of life,
Who spin all their worries, embracing the strife.
From chaos, we bloom, like flowers in spring,
With laughter, we build our own throne and we sing!

Revelations on Ruined Roads

With a flat tire here and a wobbly seat,
I'm off on a trip, can't handle the heat.
The GPS glitches, insists I go west,
While I'm heading for dreams, and just failing the test.

Through puddles and potholes, I dance with the fate,
Lost in the chaos, still feeling quite great.
Every offbeat adventure, a blessing blindsides,
Like finding a donut in ten broccoli bites.

With maps that are smudged, I take on the ride,
Each curve is a chuckle, a twist to my stride.
Laughing at wrong turns that lead me to gold,
In these ruined roads, I too, must be bold.

So let's toast to the bumps and the laughter they breed,
For in every mishap, it's joy that we need.
On these paths paved in jests, I'm free to rejoice,
With humor as guide, I always have a choice.

Threads of Courage in Twisted Paths

In a lane where squirrels plot,
I tripped on shoelaces, forgot.
Chasing dreams as they appeared,
Fell in puddles, laughed, and sneered.

With each turn, a new surprise,
Found a frog in a suit and ties.
He said, "Hurry, don't be late!"
I asked, "What? To mate with fate?"

My compass spun like a top,
Guiding me to a pancake shop.
Flip the flapjacks, take a chance,
Life's a long, wobbly dance!

So I stride through this strange terrain,
Laughing hard, ignoring pain.
With courage sewn in every seam,
Who knew life's path was so extreme?

The Quest Beyond Comfort

Sipped my coffee in a haze,
Dreamed of adventure-filled days.
Hopped into my trusty car,
It broke down—now I'm a star!

Not the star I hoped to be,
Just a meme for all to see.
Next to llamas, I felt quite bold,
"This isn't in the plans!" I told.

On the road, I danced with fate,
A raccoon stole my lunch plate.
I chased him down through weeds and muck,
Found my purpose—oh, what luck!

In discomfort, I found my roll,
Sat on thorns, but still felt whole.
Each twist and turn, a laugh or two,
Life's a ride, with a lovely view!

Lessons Carved in Stone and Sand

With a map drawn in crayon wax,
I set sail to find the facts.
Tripped on stones, my shoes went fly,
In slow motion, oh my my!

Wrote my lessons in the sand,
But waves had other plans in hand.
They washed away my smart ideas,
Leaving only: face your fears.

In the quarry, rocks would laugh,
"Hey, kid, take the scenic path!"
I stumbled on a pebble crew,
"Let's learn to dance!" they shouted too.

So I grooved among the boulders,
With some laughter, strength unfolds here.
Each misstep, a step to sway,
In life's dance, we find our way!

Horizons Obliterated by Doubt

Peered at morning, fog so thick,
Doubts like squirrels, playful trick.
Thought I knew where to ascend,
Ended up in a cat's pretend.

With my checklist all a mess,
Took the path of total stress.
A chicken crossed to make me pause,
Clucked, "Are you without a cause?"

In shadows, questions chased the light,
Am I lost, or is this right?
A friend's dog showed me the way,
Pants and howls—now let's play!

So I waved my doubt goodbye,
With disbelief, I learned to fly.
Humor helped to clear the haze,
Embrace the bumps and laugh for days!

The Highway of Discontent

On the road with potholes wide,
My GPS is lost inside.
With every turn, I hit a wall,
Laughing hard, I start to crawl.

Mile markers dance in silly styles,
I wave at cows, they seem to smile.
Detours lead to ice cream stands,
I skip my route and eat with hands.

Street signs shout in jumbled tongues,
Each wrong turn gives me new lungs.
With laughter echoed by the breeze,
I'll take the paths that help me seize.

So here's to maps with missing parts,
Adventures bloom from broken charts.
Though my ride is far from neat,
I'm kicking up some fun, with feet!

Broken Roads to Revelation

Bumpy paths, oh what a trip,
Every twist makes coffee sip.
I dodge the mud and fly through air,
My car just laughed, "You think I care?"

With flat tires and a chuckle too,
I ponder life, what's best to do?
I stop to dance with frogs on leaves,
They croak the answers, 'Just believe!'

A sign says, 'One way to the truth,'
But it led me straight to a boot.
My compass points to wibbly-wobbly,
But that just means it's time to hobble.

So I'll embrace this scenic plight,
On broken roads, I'll find the light.
Each bump a laugh, each dip a cheer,
Life's lesson learned in every gear!

Steps Through the Ashes

Each step I take, there's ash and dust,
But I belly flop in every gust.
My shoes are worn, my shirt's askew,
With playful fire, I dance and boo.

Through embers glowing, I skip and slide,
My missteps turn into a joyride.
With each leap, I find new grace,
Excitement paints a silly face.

The path is rough, the smoke a joke,
Yet laughter bursts like fearless smoke.
I trip on dreams left in the air,
And haul my heart—what a wild affair!

So here's to ashes, warm and bright,
They spark my soul, ignite my sight.
In every stumble, I laugh and climb,
Finding purpose in a silly rhyme!

Torn Pages of a Lifebook

In a book with pages ripped and torn,
I find new plots where dreams are born.
Characters dancing in mischief cheer,
With every flip, I shed a tear.

The ink may smudge, the words may fade,
But these wild tales will never trade.
Each line a giggle, each plot a twist,
I scribble joy, can't let it miss!

Chapters claim they'll make me wise,
But oh what fun in silly lies!
I pen my fables, with doodles bright,
In this ragged tale, I find my light.

So here's to pages worn with flair,
With laughter spilling everywhere.
As I scribble life, both bold and free,
I know its purpose is glee for me!

Stories Woven in the Wind

Once I found a map in the attic,
But it led me to a pile of static.
Chased a rooster for a golden egg,
Only found my lunch; it was a leg!

With my compass spinning 'round and round,
It pointed north, but I went southbound.
Met a squirrel who claimed to be wise,
He asked for nuts and spouted lies.

Tried to surf on a borrowed lawn chair,
Tipped and fell; my splash was rare.
Thought I'd take an easy train ride,
Ended up on a roller coaster slide!

Through tangled trails and mishap's glow,
I laughed till I cried, 'cause that's how it goes.
For in this chaos, I found delight,
That life's a jest, painted in bright light!

A Canvas of Uncertainty

I painted goals with colors so bold,
But my brush slipped; I was left in the cold.
I tried to sketch a path to the stars,
But I ended up doodling funny cars.

Each line a wobbly twist and shout,
With splashes of paint that I swirled about.
Thought I'd create a masterpiece neat,
Instead made a mess; oh, isn't that sweet?

An artist's face made of spaghetti,
Goes to show this life can be petty.
Though the canvas might not come out right,
I giggle aloud, what a humorous sight!

Lost in the swirl of bright, tangled threads,
I embrace the chaos, ignore all the dreads.
For in every stroke, laughter draws near,
Life's funny when you let go of your fear!

Lighthouses in the Dark

In the midst of night, my GPS failed,
The only light was a cat that wailed.
I stumbled on rocks, tripped over my shoes,
Thought I was wise, turns out I'm just bruised.

A lighthouse shone, but only at noon,
Where I mistook a raccoon for a moon.
It winked at me, with mischief in its eye,
Said, "Follow my lead, don't be shy!"

Navigating stars that danced out of tune,
I asked a seagull, "Can I borrow your swoon?"
But it flapped its wings and flew off in haste,
Leaving me lost with time to waste.

Yet in the dark, the giggles ignite,
For those silly troubles make the moments bright.
Each detour a story, every laugh a spark,
In this crazy journey, we're all lighthouses in the dark!

Fragments of Hope

I wandered into a thrift shop of dreams,
Picked up a globe; it didn't have seams.
Spun it around, tried to plan my next move,
But it pointed to snacks, my hunger to soothe.

I met a wise old sock in a drawer,
Claimed to hold secrets of life, just a score.
With stitches and threads that told a tale,
Said, "Wear me tight, you'll never fail!"

Thought I'd sail past clouds on a kite,
But the wind was rude, gave me quite the fright.
Plummeting down with a splat and a screech,
Found solace in laughter; it's the best kind of reach.

So here's to the stumbles, the fun and the slips,
Fragments of hope are my joyful scripts.
In the chaos, I gather each lesson and cheer,
For the ride might be bumpy, but the joy is right here!

Carnival of Choices

Step right up, don't be shy,
Just spin the wheel, give it a try!
Clowns with dreams in funky shoes,
Pick a path, which one to choose?

Balloons that float, a mirror maze,
Life's a game, full of delays.
Toss a ring, can't find the prize,
Laugh and sigh as time flies by.

Cotton candy clouds swirl around,
In this funhouse, lost can be found.
A rollercoaster of hopes and fears,
Who knew choices could bring such cheers?

So grab a friend, let's take a chance,
In this carnival, join the dance!
With every twist, a chuckle waits,
Life's a circus with wacky fates.

Undercurrents of Dreaming

Waves of laughter crash and roll,
Dreams are surfboards, take a stroll.
Diving deep in silly schemes,
Paddle on, follow those beams.

Fish wear hats, they swim on by,
Tangled nets, give it a try.
Each swell's a giggle, a slip, a slide,
In underwater worlds, laughter abides.

Mermaids giggle, and seaweed sways,
Finding anchors in crazy ways.
Follow the bubbles, don't be shy,
Float along, let your spirit fly.

Life's a splash, a slippery game,
With every dive, you're never the same.
Surf the kooky, ride the tides,
In this ocean, joy confides.

Signs Along a Winding Road

Zigzag lanes, each turn a tease,
Watch for signs like quirky pleas.
"Detour ahead", but where's that go?
Lost in laughter, don't move too slow.

"Avoid potholes, but trip with glee,"
Erratic maps, what's the key?
Each corner hides some funny plight,
Roads of nonsense, oh what a sight!

Bumpy rides and bright billboards,
"Pick a destination," the mind rewards.
Finding joy in every stumble,
Twisting paths make the heart rumble.

Fuel up on fun, heed the jest,
In this road trip, you're a guest.
So grab your snacks and a drink or two,
The ride of life's made just for you.

Tears of Transformation

A sobbing caterpillar's plight,
Wants to fly but can't find the light.
Wrapped in dreams, the world feels tight,
Silly cries turn into flight.

Shedding layers, what a fuss,
Moths have parties without us!
Fluttering past the gloomy days,
Transforming tears into golden rays.

Through the struggles, giggles grow,
Watch out world, I'm ready to glow!
From puddles of tears, blooms arise,
Life's a joke wrapped in surprise.

So when you feel the weight of woe,
Remember the dance, just let it flow.
Laughter lights a path so bright,
In tears, find the wings for flight.

Echoes in the Wilderness

In the woods I took a stroll,
Tripped on roots, lost my goal.
A squirrel laughed, said, 'Oh dear!'
I waved back, still full of cheer.

Branches slap, they whisper low,
'Where's he off to? Don't you know?'
With each step, I search and frown,
But the trees just giggle down.

My map's a riddle, what a bore,
'Just go left!' it said before.
I followed right, oh what a tease,
Now I'm lost among the leaves.

Still I dance, with every stumble,
Through this chaos, I won't grumble.
For in the wilds, I find my tune,
With the moon above, I'm over the moon.

A Tapestry of Trials

I tried to weave my life so grand,
But tangled yarn, it slipped my hand.
Weaving dreams, I made a knot,
Said, 'Who knew it could be so fraught?'

I spilt my tea on that fine thread,
Creating art, or so I said.
With each slip, I laugh and cheer,
Turns out chaos is quite sincere.

Life's a patchwork, colors blend,
With every stitch, I must pretend.
For every hole, a story told,
Of upturned plans and dreams gone bold.

So I wear this quilt, embrace the mess,
Each flaw a tale, a laugh, no less.
In this clumsy fabric, I stake my claim,
For every bump, it's all a game.

The Grail Beyond the Horizon

Chasing glory, what a treat!
I thought I'd find it on the street.
But every sign points me away,
Seems my grail's gone, gone astray.

I climbed a hill, thought I was near,
But found a goat instead, oh dear!
He chewed my map with such delight,
Now I'm the one who's lost sight!

The quest is silly, full of twists,
Like battling air, it doesn't exist.
But every tumble, every plight,
Leads to laughter in the night.

So I'll march forth, paint the skies,
With every fail, a new surprise.
The treasure's joy, wrapped in a smile,
Each bump a dance, I'll walk a mile.

Footprints in the Fog

In the fog, I tread so light,
Tripping o'er shadows, what a sight!
Footprints echo, lost from view,
Is that my shoe? Or maybe two?

Mist swirls around and plays its game,
Each step I take, it knows my name.
It giggles soft, 'You're on your way!'
But where to now? Oh, where to stay?

I zigzag here, I bounce back there,
Who knew wandering could be so rare?
In this muddy maze, my thoughts run wild,
Like every moment, a playful child.

So I laugh at paths I never take,
With every trip, I learn to shake.
In this fog, I find my dance,
For life's a jest, a whirl, a chance.

Searching for the North Star

I set out one day with a map in my hand,
Thought I'd find fame, then sip on life's brand.
But GPS failed, and I lost my way,
Now I'm stuck in a field with a cow named Ray.

I wandered through forests, climbed every hill,
Seeking direction, I tripped on a quill.
The North Star's a myth, they told me with glee,
Guess I'll just follow this squirrel up a tree.

With snacks in my pocket, I wander and roam,
Each path that I take feels like far from home.
But laughter's my compass, it leads me with grace,
As I stumble through life, a comedic embrace.

So here's to the journeys both silly and bold,
Where dreams turn to laughs and the truth is retold.
Forget about maps, I'm in it for fun,
Just chasing my tail, under bright shining sun.

The Weight of Expectations

They say I should excel, climb mountains so tall,
But each time I try, I just seem to fall.
A job in the clouds and a house made of dreams,
Turns into a loaf of burnt toast, it seems.

My friends all grow up, they've got suits and high skills,
While I'm here in my PJs, with snacks and good thrills.
They ask me my plans, I just shrug and I grin,
Life's weight feels lighter with a joke and a spin.

Each boulder of pressure, I toss like a ball,
Instead of a titan, I'm a jester, that's all.
I'll dance through my failures with style and flair,
While wearing my awkwardness like it's couture wear.

So here's to the pressure, I'm laughing out loud,
In a world full of checklists, I'm dancing unbowed.
Expectations may loom, but I'll take them in stride,
With a wink and a grin, on this wild, wobbly ride.

Bridges Over Troubled Waters

I built me a bridge made of spaghetti and hope,
Thought it would hold, but I struggled to cope.
With each step I took, a noodle would snap,
Then I'm splashed in the river, all covered in crap.

They told me to cross, I aimed for the stars,
But the bridge turned to mush, I fell into jars.
My goals started floating, bobbing in waves,
While I waved to the fish, who were laughing at knaves.

So I grabbed a flotilla made out of old dreams,
But it sunk like my chances, or so it sure seems.
Yet laughter's the anchor, it keeps me afloat,
As I paddle my way on this jiggly boat.

So if life is a river, and troubles abound,
I'm a pirate of joy, treasure's here to be found.
With a smile on my face and jokes lined up tight,
I'll sail through the waves, finding joy in the fight.

Cracks in the Armor of Purpose

With a shiny suit of armor, I thought I was grand,
But the cracks in my shield came from slipping in sand.
I strutted and preened, said, 'Look how I shine!'
Then tripped on my ego, and fell on some pine.

The more that I shine, the more I can see,
That purpose is messy; it's not just for me.
With each awkward tumble, I gather my pride,
Like leaves in the fall, they just float by my side.

So I gather these cracks like badges of fun,
Each one tells a tale, each one's surely won.
For purpose lies hidden in tumbles and slips,
In laughter and joy, in the world's funny quips.

So let's toast to the journey, the stumbles, the falls,
With cracks in my armor, I'll still stand up tall.
For each little mishap that makes people chime,
Is just life's way of saying, 'You're doing just fine!'

Bandages of Experience

I took a step, then tripped and fell,
A patchwork of lessons, oh what a swell!
I'm wrapped in bandages, a colorful sight,
Learning while laughing, not fleeing in fright.

Every bruise has a story that tickles my vein,
Like that time on the bus, I danced on a train.
Life's a carousel, spinning with glee,
With bumps in the road just a part of the spree.

I stumble, I tumble, I giggle and grin,
Life's slapstick comedy, thick skin's where it's been.
No smooth sailing here, just gleeful tai chi,
I'm sailing on laughter, come bounce along with me!

So here's to the bandages, the laughter, the cheer,
I gather up moments, no space for the fear.
I'll wear my adventures like badges of pride,
With each twist and turn, a fun-loving ride!

When Thorns Become Roses

Pricked by the thorns but I laugh and sway,
Each scratch a reminder, come join in the play!
I find all the roses but trip on the vine,
And when I look up, I'm stuck on cloud wine.

Bumbling along, I give plants my best care,
Who knew that a cactus could offer such flair?
With every misstep, I gather more cheer,
It's not such a struggle, when you're grinning ear to ear.

Petals in hand but the thorns in my back,
I wear them like jewels in this whimsical track.
Like a cat in a bag, I've learned to embrace,
The hiccups in life, oh, what a fine race!

So here's to the struggle, the fun in the mess,
To find the sweet joy in the thorns, I confess.
All prickles aside, let your laughter compose,
Life's funny bouquet when thorns become rose!

Between Heartbeats

In the quiet moments, I trip over time,
Between heartbeats and hiccups, I dance to the rhyme.
When life skips a beat, I cartwheel with glee,
Who needs a smooth page in the book that is me?

The pauses, the gasps, they make a great plot,
I fumble through life, oh, is it all for naught?
But a chuckle or two makes the bumps brighter still,
Like a rubber band story—stretch it at will!

I gather my heartbeats like colorful beads,
Some are quite funky, like my best friend's deeds.
A tango with chaos, we laugh and we cheer,
Between heartbeats' thumps, there's always a leer!

So here's to the moments that catch us off guard,
We find them amusing and don't play them hard.
In the rhythm of life, let your laughter outshine,
Between the heartbeats, you'll find the divine!

The Inner Odyssey

Oh, the treasure maps that lead me astray,
With twists and with turns, I giggle away.
Through valleys of waffles and mountains of pie,
My inner odyssey makes me laugh 'til I cry.

Each fork in the road, a riddle or jest,
My compass keeps spinning; oh, isn't that best?
I wear my confusion like socks that don't match,
In this wild expedition, it's all I can catch.

With dreams as my ship, and hopes for a sail,
I navigate waters where laughter prevails.
I've bumped into whales, they chuckle with glee,
In this wacky adventure, there's always a key!

So set sail with me on this uncharted spree,
With fun as my anchor, I'm wild and I'm free.
For chaos and laughter, a glorious blend,
The inner odyssey, where giggles transcend!

Pathways Unraveled

I took a left where I should have gone right,
Now I'm lost in a cafe, feeling quite light.
The map in my hand is just a big joke,
I asked for directions, got a laugh and a poke.

Every step I take seems to lead me astray,
I tripped on a squirrel who stole my parfait.
With each twist and turn, I find more to learn,
Like how to bargain with pigeons for bread that's not burned.

I bumped into a tree that claimed to be wise,
It told me to follow the birds in the skies.
But the skies were grey, and the birds all sang,
They left me bewildered, feeling quite tang.

Yet here I am, with laughter on cue,
Armed with my snacks and a thirst for the new.
Life's a car ride with friends all a-squeal,
On roads made of waffles, a surreal meal.

Tangled Roads of Becoming

I started on a road, but the map was a riddle,
With a sign that read 'Go straight' but played a fiddle.
A roundabout appeared, singing a tune,
I danced my way through like a carefree buffoon.

The GPS said, 'Turn left!' but I turned with flair,
And ended up munching on cotton candy in air.
Each path is a circus, a juggling of dreams,
Balloons fly away with the craziest themes.

With every detour, I made a new friend,
A llama on a bicycle, what a godsend!
It winked as it pedaled, a sight to behold,
Its wisdom? "Life's fun--don't do what you're told!"

So here's to the wanderers, lost in delight,
Making mistakes, like it's our birthright.
Each twist and each turn is a dance or a clatter,
In the zigzag of life, we find what matters.

Threads of Destiny Woven

I tried to stitch patterns with all of my might,
But ended up tangled in yarn day and night.
With needles that danced to a rhythm so strange,
The fabric of fate laughed at my clumsy change.

Each thread that I pulled took me somewhere else,
Like a sock puppet parade, or a dollhouse of elves.
I knitted 'wisdom' that unraveled all day,
A scarf with a twist that led me astray.

I thought it was cozy, a wrap for my heart,
But the stitches were wobbly, a true work of art.
"Wear it with pride!" said the kitten of fate,
"Who cares 'bout the size when you're feeling great?"

So here in the chaos, I find my tight knit,
With laughter and joy, I embrace every bit.
The threads may be messy, but they're all mine,
In this tapestry amusing, I feel just divine!

Bumps on the Trail of Insight

I packed up my bags, ready for the hike,
But forgot my good shoes and brought just a spike.
With every small bump, my foot would protest,
Each stumble a lesson, though not the best quest.

I tripped over rocks that whispered and chuckled,
They said, "You ain't ready, your luggage is buckled!"
With branches that poked and grass that was sly,
I learned how to tumble, how not to deny.

A rabbit appeared, with a map upside down,
It winked and it wobbled, wore a tiny crown.
"Follow me closely, I know where to go,
Just watch for the mud, it has plans of its own!"

Thus each little bump on this path I embrace,
With humor and charm, I keep up the pace.
Life's about stumbles, those silly old slips,
While finding our insights, we're all taking trips!

www.ingramcontent.com/pod-product-compliance
Lightning Source LLC
Chambersburg PA
CBHW051633160426
43209CB00004B/631